ANCHOR BOOKS

EXPRESSIONS FOR A NEW CENTURY FROM THE MIDLANDS

Edited by

Steve Twelvetree

First published in Great Britain in 2000 by
ANCHOR BOOKS
Remus House,
Coltsfoot Drive,
Woodston,
Peterborough, PE2 9JX
Telephone (01733) 898102

HB ISBN 1 85930 784 1
SB ISBN 1 85930 789 2

FOREWORD

Anchor Books is a small press, established in 1992, with the aim of promoting readable poetry to as wide an audience as possible. We see ourselves as a platform for new and established poets to built upon their talents and see their work in print for possibly the first time.

Each of the chosen poems has been specifically favoured from a large selection of entries sent. As always the editing proved to be a difficult task and as the edition, the final selection was mine.

Expressions For A New Century From The Midlands is a unique collection of poetry and verse written in a variety of styles and themes, brought to us from many of today's modern and traditional writers, who reside in this area. The poems are easy to relate to and encouraging to read, offering engaging entertainment to their reader.

This delightful collection is sure to win your heart, making it a companion for life and perhaps even earning that favourite little spot upon your bookshelf.

Steve Twelvetree
Editor

CONTENTS

LOVE FOREVER

Love is a serenade
  from the very soul
No rapturous sonnet
  ever sung so sweet
Soft melody of a mystic
  charm
Love brings to pain -
  untroubled sleep.

Love is a hymnal -
  God divine
Ingredient blessed at
  His table stand
Love, Heaven's nectar
  of purest wine
Offered to all by His
  own loving hand.

Love is a healer of purest
  balm
His most precious gift -
  for everyone
Love is the crucifixion
  sign -
Love is forgiveness that
  goes on and on.

Mary Skelton

PAUPER'S GOLD

Blues and purple in a golden sky
reflect the brightness
in vision's eye.
Watching the sun slowly fade
shadow hues pass tree-lined glades.
A cast-down look does not see
the sunset glow in such majesty.
For nothing could compare
to this pauper's gold,
each changing colour attracts and holds.
Wealth so rich - could be no curse
blind are those so full in purse,
they do not see this talking sky
this golden wonder
they pass by!

H Lewis

GREEDY DOG

This dog will eat anything
Wobbly spaghetti
Paper confetti
Red chilli
Or your friend Lily
A big fat fly
Or your dad's best tie
He will eat your chips
Or your felt tips
A yellow peg
Or a big pink egg
A plastic toy gun
Or a baker bun
This dog will eat anything
Except for mushrooms or cucumber
Now, what is wrong with those, I wonder.

Jodie Price (9)

REMEMBER ME

Remember me when I am gone,
No longer on the earth.
Remember me from time to time,
My value and my worth.

Remember me in time to come,
For what I did, not left undone.
Remember me and when you do,
You will feel the love I have for you.

Remember me with just a smile,
Will make my living all worthwhile.
Remember now we cannot touch,
There is more to life, so very much.

Remember now you cannot see,
We loved each other you and me.
Remember now you cannot hear,
With a loving thought I am always near.

Remember as you walk your ground,
I am with you all around,
And when the coming time is right,
With love that binds we will again unite.

Carole Wood

A SECRET PLACE

I have a secret place inside my mind.
I keep it there for me,
Where no one else can find
The treasures that I store there year by year,
To take out, now and then,
To bring a smile or tear.

Past mem'ries there cascade around my head;
O'er faces, places, time,
Far countries, my mind's led
And then, at times of happiness or doubt,
I can relive the joys
These mem'ries bring about.

This is a secret place
Which can a lifetime's story hold;
This is a secret place
Far, far beyond the price of gold.

Sheila E Harvey

A MORNING IN JANUARY

The wide, white width of the seagulls' wings,
Imprinted against the low, ominous sky,
The sudden gust, the sleet that stings,
Ladies' skirts billowing, wild and high.
Quiet-eyed sheep in furrowed brown field,
Huddled for refuge among spiky hedgerows
Nibbling, carefully searching for the first green yield.
Tormented wires screeching overhead,
The shrill, strident call from the electric train,
Heavy traffic's constant hum, shrieking brakes,
Flapping coat, slapping scarf, face and fingers
Tingling with pain, eyes watering, nose dripping,
Wet boots heavy on aching feet.
As I turn for home, laughing with relief leaning back on
The wind that is sweeping me on, I feel warm and light
Like a crisp dancing leaf as I am cradled, urged and pushed along.
I stumble through the doorway, flopping into a chair, my hair
Tumbled about me, cheeks all aglow, feeling clean and refreshed,
The trees in the garden sway low, bowing in farewell, but I swear,
The wind sounds bereft.

Doreen Roys

CITY 2000

Bleep! 'CU at 3?' Text Message
Requesting human company.
Square-eyed, brain-fried, city slicker
Responds with E-mail (is it quicker?)
Cybercafé cappuccino
Downed in ten, then back to business.
Videoconference with Japan
Talking screens leave boardrooms banned.
MDs, FDs head for home.
Hour hand's heavy, silent phones.
Neon lights and trendy bars
Beckon lonely workers' hearts.
Forgotten family left to wait
For mobile phones 'Home by 8'
Blank-faced, straight-laced (more like 9)
Returns home. Empty bottle of wine.
Low fat, TV dinner for one
Microwaved. Tastes like foam.
Kids, grown up during office hours.
Say goodnight. Sleeping flowers.
Trawl the net, check for mail,
Life on hold, connection failed.
Day done, night gone, up at 5
Disk inserted in A drive.
Crawls in, warm bed. Reluctant sleep.
Eventual switch off . . . Alarm. *Bleep!*

Frances Pallett

AUTUMN

Nature's chemistry has painted umbrella trees,
Yellow, red and orange their autumn leaves.
Sapless now, they gently fall, carpeting the woodland floor:
Flowers freed from winter's thaw will blossom in the spring once more.

Heralds of summer, birds have flown
From gossamer shrouded woodland home:
Still silence on the autumn heath:
Crackling dead leaves beneath our feet.

Death black crows; black beady-eyed,
Croak death knell to summer in the autumn skies:
In Arley's churchyard, Genesis cedars grow
From gnarled cracked bark gum resins flow.

Arthritic villagers beneath churchyard land
Where doe-eyed cherubs, cold crosses stand:
Chrysanthemums patchwork their green moss bed,
Drinking sweet rain from pitcher jars of lead.

Edward L G Holmes

BE MINE

Hey baby, unsheathe them claws
all sharpened, on the delicate flesh of boys
tear off my ageing, wrinkled skin
layer by layer, expose the child within
cast me back through realms of time
rip away them lonely years
    be mine!
Engulf me, in your well of eternal fire
encourage these feeble attempts
to satisfy your yearning desire
    be my destiny!
And if finesse is lacking, then teach me
show me, how to make you sigh
show me, how to make you cry
show me, that tender place upon your thigh
show me, how to die
    be my dream!
Be every waking thing I have not seen
take me places, only you have been
guide me to the depths of your every need
teach me baby, show me where to feed
    be my lover!
Tell me when you need a gentle touch
a gentle kiss, a brush of lips
or maybe a little rougher
tell me, just how much
    be cruel!
    Be good!
    Be bad!
    Be . . . you!

Jeff Mitchell

A POTION FOR THE SOUL

Reach love in;
that we may find ourselves
enwrapped by your truth.
We peel away layers
excited to see the revelations,
　　　　to feel each colour,
　　　　live the shining brightness,
experience the excitement love dictates.
Strengthened, we explore illicit depths.
Enticed, we delve in danger's poison
slowly forging our bonds,
tasting the bitterness of consequence.
Love has no distance too great
　　no separation too long;
though souls suffer, wander
in waves of need and memory,
where boundaries of anything fall away
from us giving and receiving the potion.
With love a neuter where the wrong?
The sting still is the rightfulness of
true love which ties
past, present, future in tighter knots.
The pain for caring -　　damnation.
　　　　For our souls - thought.
We are what we are.

Mary Percival

CAVES FIELD

For many years this treasured ground
Has served our village well.
But now, to everyone's dismay
It is proposed to sell

This last green space for building land.
Why does this have to be?
Man cannot live by bread alone
He needs variety.

Here we can watch a cricket match
And children playing ball.
Why should this pleasant field be doomed
When it is loved by all?

What is a village if it has
No place for sport or play?
Why should some outside folk decide
Our future in this way?

So we shall fight to try to keep
Our ancient cricket field,
And hope our voices will be heard
Before its fate is sealed.

Kay Gilbert

THE ESSEX COUNTRY CHURCH

A fair county is this eastern realm
That slopes muddily to the sea,
Its countryside dotted with oak and elm
That has long served humanity.

And man to God began to praise
By building churches to be found
With spires and towers that point and raise
God's house heavenbound.

Across wide fields of ripening wheat
Or down a winding willowy lane,
Amongst the clustered trees a distant peep
Of flinty tower or shiny weather vane.

From famous Greensted's oaken walls
To Thaxted's glorious spire
The traveller will want to pause,
Reflect, explore and admire.

But it is the humbler church, less understood,
That is typical of this region
With tower and belfry made of wood
Whilst shingled spires are legion.

From pretty Stock to Doddinghurst,
Blackmore to Margaretting,
Each village has a lovely church,
Lambourn and Navestock not forgetting.

Through the history in its walls
Of brick or flint or timber,
Or standing beside moated halls
The Essex church will be remembered.

A L Lawrence

THE SUNSET PATH

May I walk once more down that winding path,
Through the green, green fields and the hedgerows tall,
By the lofty trees which probe the sky,
And listen to the cuckoo's call;
To cross again the little white bridge
Which spans the placid watercress stream,
Where cowslips grow in the moistured ground
And blend with the kingcups' golden gleam.

Then where the stream grows and swells
And comes to a water gathering bend;
Here as boys we dived and swam,
Never dreaming that youth could end;
But now I dwell in nostalgic age
And memory performs those feats again,
Why not? If we still remember them
Our vigours of youth were not in vain.

And so to the spinney and with grassy path
Where pigeons coo and the chaffinch sings,
The woodland flowers their carpets lay,
And the toadstools form their magic rings;
I know of a nearby badger set,
I've seen a dog fox loping by,
And watched a kestrel hover and dive
In a cloudless, sunlit, summer sky.

I've watched the sun go westering down
In a splendour of crimson and gold,
And idly reflected that everyone
Must wax, and wane, and grow old,
But watching that breathless beauty,
And the lengthening shadows fall,
I hope life's evening perhaps may be
The most beautiful time of all!

Bernard Laughton

UNIVERSITY CHALLENGE

Your Uni years are beginning
Make the most of every day
New home, new friends, new way of life
Will help you on your way,
Revise the grades, achieve your aim
With friends around you doing the same,
Go ahead! Don't cramp your style
In the end it will be worthwhile,
Study and learning, so much to be done
Good luck, be happy, take care, have fun.

We will all miss you, but in our thoughts you'll be
No shopping trips together, no creeping in at three,
No bathroom paraphernalia
No music on full blast
And those noisy parties
I hope they were the last
An empty bed, wardrobes bare
Cuddly toys left on the chair,
Those way-out clothes and clumpy shoes
The disco nights and barbecues.

It's all so quiet now you have gone
But times do change and life goes on,
Just a few lines in a letter
Or a phone call when you're free
And if you have a problem
You know just where I'll be.

L France

THE STORM

The lightning flashes, the thunder roars,
Down comes the rain, how it pours;
It beats upon the window pane,
Creating puddles in the lane.
Lashing down through the trees,
Dark and stormy days are these.
The sky is black and low with cloud,
The lightning's bright, the thunder's loud.
It won't last long, 'twill soon be gone
And then the sun will shine again.
The gardens all were very dry,
They needed that rain from on high.
Don't begrudge them what they need
We all need our growth to feed.
With nurturing we too will show
That like the flowers we can grow.

Ruth Smith

MY PET HAMSTER

I have a pet hamster
Fluffy is his name
He sometimes climbs onto my head.
Then gets real comfy as if it's his bed
He crawls all over my body as if it's a game
Up my sleeves and trouser legs
He tickles with his feet
Sniffing and touching with his cold nose
I don't think I can take much more of this
So back into his cage he goes.

Marc-Ross Beeching (10)

WAR

The sands of time are but a dream
The reality of true human nature is at war amongst its brothers.
To let your thoughts, not ours conquer
Time now must be at a standstill.

We must wait for you to come to us,
Only then can the peace of the land of our fathers
Once again be as one

This time you must believe us for you will not have that time again.
Stand still and watch, and learn, we are the only ones
Who can bring peace.

A hand is held out and the sign of love to you is sent,
The skylark flies above
But dark are the times ahead for those that argue.
You cannot change the source from which it comes,
But you can help stop the flow of hate from those that sent it.

Return it not for even though they do you wrong,
They believe in what they do.
Do not chastise but bend with forgiveness.
Hate is too strong, a powerful force in itself.
You must hold out a hand that's true.
Not all are evil. Only a small band of disbelievers.

The world must have peace, it is on our shoulders alone
To bear this hatred. But yours to give out love.

Let it run else the seas will run dry before it's too late.
Tell the world *stop* let us get out of here,
We want peace not war.

J Bentley

TWO FRIENDS OF MINE

Esther and Sue we shared one thing
The big 'C' - their time was short
But how they used it to the limit
And allowed no cloud to dim it -

After the treatment it was - pick up the threads
And get on with life - it's like gold.
No time to waste - it's too precious to squander
There's so much to do - be bold.

Esther became a companion to a frail old lady
She bought a little car to get them about
How they enjoyed it - friends to visit and have tea
Then she did a trip to New Zealand - relatives to see.

Sue arranged trips abroad to Italy and France
She opened doors for us to explore, and it wasn't by chance
That to the Hotel Dieu she took us to view - it's a hospice at Beanne
Chapel and ward combined - prayers every three hours - two to a
bed so not alone.

They touched a lot of lives and made friends wherever they went
Helped others to see and do - things beyond their dreams
They're remembered with love and their time was well spent
And they gave us memories to treasure - with pleasure.

Myrtle E Holmes

MY TWIN SISTER

I have a twin sister
Identical to me
No one knows her
As well as I do
She knows when I'm sad
She knows when I'm glad
For she is the other half of me.

Ella Wright

MY ANGELS

Oh my life, they're at it again
The quarrelling, the fighting, they're driving me insane
If I could have one lie in, it would be such a treat
But no chance of that, as they jump from bed to feet.

The clattering, the banging, why do they make such a noise
Can't they do it quietly, when they're playing with their toys
Running bathroom taps, and flushing the toilet chain
I never knew it made such noise, as it gushes through the drain.

I reach out for my pillow, and plonk it on my head
Then they burst into the bedroom, and jump upon my bed
I give them all a hug, and they disappear down stairs
One, two, three, I'm glad they're not in pairs.

I stumble out of bed, my eyes just little slits
The clock says seven thirty, this really is the pits
I make it to the shower, as I hear voices raised once more
I shout, 'Can someone let the dog out before he dribbles on the floor.'

In and out the shower, turban round my head
Still feel exhausted, have I really been to bed?
Downstairs all is quiet, as they watch TV and eat
It won't last long though, before they're scuttling round my feet.

Door open, the dog bounds in with glee
Muddy paws on my dressing gown, as he makes a fuss of me
Postman delivers the letters, and they all run to the door
I shake my head in silence, as they start again once more.

A typical Saturday morning, another hectic day
As they race to find their clothes, so they can go out to play
But I wouldn't change a single thing, God gave them me to keep
My little rascals in the morning, my little angels when they sleep.

Angelina Marsh

THE GREATEST GIFT

The greatest gift I know, is love
It's a gift that's sent from heaven above,
You will use this gift throughout your days
In many, many different ways.

There's the love you have for Father and Mother,
There's the love you have for sister and brother,
And through this love you can only gain,
It keeps you strong when there is pain.

Then when you meet your partner for life,
There's the love which exists between husband and wife.
It keeps you going through good times and bad,
When you are happy or when you are sad.

Then there's the love you have for your child,
Who lies there helpless, feeble and mild,
Through all the years as up they grow,
From you to them your love does flow.

The greatest gift you'll ever know,
Will come to you and make you glow,
For Christ who lives in heaven above,
Has sent to us the gift of love.

Jim Harrap

THE BUSINESSMAN

The man is bored with the quiet of the office.
He needs to go to another land.
This is the last resort.
He has finished with the designer labels.
The drinks and lunches with the boss.
Far away across the seas, escape.
Where there are plenty of poor.
Many girls in many clubs.
Making full use of their conversational skills.
Compensation for the lack of education.
They listen to the men talking about their wives at home.
Mocking the fact that they like sewing.
While the bright lights of the city lure the sad men.
The men dance on the many disco floors.
The hospitality girls laugh at their clients.

Nicholas Thompson

TURN AROUND

Turn the words around,
the words that make the sounds,
that fall from your lips,
which tumble from thought's grip.

Twist the sight you see,
the view you see of me,
move your vision's sight,
turn dark thoughts into light.

Move forward with your life,
towards happiness from your strife,
hope must be your end,
turn your thoughts around my friend.

David Buck

FISHING

When everyday things start to get you down,
Don't sit and wear a frown.
Dig for some worms, get some bread,
Oh yes and don't forget a maggot or two.
Get a rod and some line,
Let everyday things go from your mind.
Really sit down and unwind,
Look at the beauty that's all around.
There's big fish in this pond they say,
I've seen some jump across the way.
Just cast your float and sit and wait.
If come the end of the day,
No fish has took your bait,
Just remember there's always another day.

David Frost

GRANDPA'S GREENHOUSE

Cobwebs hanging from the walls,
Tall ferns growing on the floor.
Weeds and algae everywhere
Bags of compost by the door.

Plant pots all in crooked piles,
Sweet jar full of seeds to sow.
Bulbs and penknife in the drawer,
Watering cans in a row.

An old decrepit sideboard,
Harbouring spiders and dust.
Seed trays ready for the spring,
Garden tools covered in rust.

Ancient remedies for germs,
Windows caked with dust and grime.
Such a state the place is in
Some would say it was a crime.

But flowers of every kind he grows,
Healthy, well formed plants are they.
Tomatoes too, sweet and juicy
And weeds as well, I have to say.

Joyce Wakefield

WINTER

Summer's nearly over
I hate the winter months
I could easily shut myself away
And wait in home patiently
For another sunny day
I hate the cold dark mornings
The bad weather that comes along the way
Oh! Be gone with you winter
Let the sun shine through your clouds of grey
Pegging out the washing
Can't feel your frost-bitten hands
Then it turns to hot aches
And your feet feel swollen
They are throbbing just like your hands
Dewdrops running off your nose
Tears streaming down your cheeks
Oh I hate the winter
It's so cold, dark and bleak.

Beverley Bozzoni

BEAUTIFUL DAY

Year 2000
New Year's Day
Wasn't like winter
It was a bright spring day.
Birds flew down
To eat the bread
I tended a plant
I thought was dead
I shook off the old leaves
Underneath there was new
The sky was so bright
The century so new.

Christine Anne Storer

SUMMERTIME

The gorgeous white fluffy trails
Of aeroplanes,
Left in a brilliant blue sky.
That's what makes me sigh
Our new baby's breath upon my face,
A very pure delight.

The warm, healing sun,
To surround me as I lie,
Takes away every worry of the day.
The sweet tweet noises of the birds
With ferocious appetites,
Make me smile on a summer's day.

A dragonfly zooms in
Its spectacular gossamer wings a-blur
It doesn't have time to stay.
As summertime is ebbing,
The steely mist closes
On a perfect day.

M Wain

BLUE DELIGHTS

God created the earth,
The air, the sea and the sky,
The latter two I find are blue,
There are also bluebirds which fly.

I come down to earth and I find
Beautiful walks, woodlands and fields,
Pathways wind on for miles and miles,
Woods have blankets of bluebells to yield.

As I walk down a country lane
A small cottage comes into view,
There's a little old lady in the garden
Dressed in the most beautiful shade of blue.

She smiles at me with twinkling blue eyes,
Behind her is well tended plot
Filled with blue cornflowers and violets,
Blue lupins and forget-me-nots.

I pause, as she glances my way,
We then enjoy a pleasant chat,
Shortly she bids me a fond farewell
As she stoops to stroke a cat.

I say goodbye to the dear little lady
As I continue down the lane,
I've enjoyed my walk very much today,
I think I'll come this way again.

Joan A Anscombe

TOGETHER

Hours, days and years slide by
but as long as I have you,
in health of body, peace of mind
as long as you are true.
Let us live unseen, unknown
never let us die,
let us steal away from this world
and tell no one where we lie.

Gill Whyman

THE LETTER

'Tis many long years since last we spoke
So now I write, and pray and hope
That you can forgive me for all this lost time
Being young and headstrong was my only crime

You cried as I left for the city of fun
Now looking back there's many stupid things I've done
Bedsits and parties, and so-called friends
But nobody there when a friend needs a friend

Now I've a son who means the world to me
Tomorrow's his first school day, how proud I'll be
I kiss his cheek, and stroke his head
He lies so peaceful in his little bed

His big day is tomorrow, he'll be excited
But beneath my smile, my heart is blighted
I will feel your tears as he walks away
Just like the tears when I left that day

So in this letter I send all my love
Asking forgiveness for things I have done
Lessons in heartache do not make me strong
Because nothing compares to the love of a mum

Pamela Mason

CLOSE THE BOOK

Angel forever stuck in the past,
in too deep, in with the sheep, once again.
Write a chapter in the book, make it last,
have a good look . . . then shut it fast, never to go back.

The feeling's so strong that it's just all wrong,
but now it's shut out and gone.
Black-iced chest, blue-iced heart,
I swear I'll never leave you, I swear we'll never part.
We'll try hard, we'll try hard and never give up.

Close the book, don't go back for another look.
Never let go,
it's gone, it's gone,
never let go,
no tiny flame burning on,
an ice-cold escape,
love cannot be let through.

In my heart, it's so wrong,
in my head the feeling's just as strong.
The flame blisters my soul and won't give up,
I try so hard yet it still burns me to dust.

Blown away into the breezes of eternity, whispering every day.
Every day . . . but,
close the book and never have another look.

The children will come out one day in sweet romantic fantasy and hope,
a fight between reality and fake, the weak are bound to break.
Brick wall, ice-cold heart and head full of farce,
you know, you know, but the ice takes over and closes the book.

I was frozen and now I'm hot, coldness of death will not close

the book for me,

All idols fall and the children cry pathetically.

The end is ice.

Sylvie Wright

STREET PARADE

Here they come, hear that drum, soldiers on parade.
Hearts beat high, girls they sigh, people all amazed.
Rhythmic feet, to the beat, all of one accord.
There they go, heel and toe, unity afford.

Heads held high, passing by, arms together swing.
Trumpets blare, children stare as to hands they cling.
Uniforms and buttons bright, eyes left, then to right.
Down the street, friends to meet, what a cheery sight.

Music sounds, gone are frowns as they march along.
Mace goes high to the sky and the sound of song
Red and gold, brave and bold, colours flying high
What a show, care laid low, troop passing by.

Thro' the town, o'er the down to the barrack square
Company halt, without fault, bravely do or dare.
Day is done, gone the sun, now's the time to rest
Drum beats tap, off goes caps, each man done his best.

Lois Burton

VIEW FROM THE LAY-BY

From the lay-by I can see
February skies all around as grey as can be
The dark skeleton of the ash tree
Almost glaring back at me
A crow flies overhead through driving rain
Going back to roost again.
An aeroplane descending low back to airport scattered with snow
Power lines first held by towers with arms a-bow.
Carry the fuel that's made at source
To bring us light and warmth of course
But I can't wait for spring and what it will bring to me to see
Green leaves on that much loved ash tree
And I am urgent for summer to arrive
It brings with it warm blue skies
with cumulus clouds drifting on high
And then comes the swallow forever on wing
I feel blessed when first I hear the nightingale sing.

Brian Holmes

SLIMMING

I've started this 'slimming' oh it's such fun
But I'd rather be munching a nice sticky bun
Can't understand how I got to this weight
Clearly it must be something I ate
Can't have any chocolate biscuits or cake
No chance of a kit-kat when it comes to break

Time to be serious I must lose a stone
Then I too can be all skin and bone
You see I really was such a big eater
But now I've got used to the taste of Ryvita
I've tried to control my calorie intake
Hopefully soon I'll be as thin as a rake

So no more big helpings of pies with a crust
Fruit, greens and crispbreads and salads a must
And if today you think I look sleek
Thank heavens for that I haven't eaten all week
I've tried really hard, bad nerves have helped too
For here I am now a trim 9 stone 2

I Jenkinson

KEEP MY EYES

Lord keep my eyes on you today
In Jesus' mighty name I pray
Keep me pure and secure
In your love forever more
Keep my eyes on the path
So I might have the last laugh
For the fear of the Lord is my treasure
And in you I'll have my pleasure

John Latimer

DEATH FOR LIFE

Full moon low, hovering still, in clouds that streak the sky,
A stark silhouette of saluting stones, in an ancient circle lie,
The sodden turf, of a worshipped hill, gropes the naked feet,
A ritual walk, this murderous night, never will he repeat.

Painted faces, chanting mouths surround the circle edge,
Consecrated blood of human heart, will seal their faithful pledge,
He is a gift, for the god, as homage for to pay,
His death ensures, nature's blessings, never fade away.

The moon she dies, but life bursts forth, Sun new born in the east,
Now struggling body, warriors drag, before the god's High Priest,
Limbs outstretched, he's tightly pinned into the altar's girth,
Unearthly screams, as tortured pain, assist the hailed one's birth.

Orange sky, dagger high, drawn downward skin to part,
From the boy's young chest, the priest arrests, the bloody
                                        pumping heart,
Words of prayer, pervade the air, in worship tribesmen call,
Amid gold and silver, textiles, pots, the most precious gift of all.

A lifeless carcass greets the Sun, his subjects now believe,
Another divine and honoured soul, through death life they receive,
The sacrificed messenger of goodwill, should aid the idol's reign,
Provide universal balance, for nature to maintain.

Christine Rooth

WINTER'S END

Last week in Feb and winter hunts on
Haunting the land till the green has all gone
A bright, crispy day, could this be spring?
But the air is so cold, your fingertips sting.

Across in the field stands a lonely bare tree
Laden with birds where its leaves should be
Their chattering songs ring loud in the air
So proud now that tree cos its branches to share.

I snatch a day's end in a sunset so clear
There's a peace in my heart you can almost hear
Hark to those birds they've something to say
'Winter is going and spring's on its way.'

Sue Comery

HALF A CENTURY

Congratulations you have reached it at last
   the age where genuine memories appear from the past
A time to look forward as well as look back
   sometimes at yourself in something you lack
A time to begin, a time to enjoy
   yet still have flash memories of yourself as a boy
Try not to let down it eats at the heart
   a lingering pain loath to part
Move on with hindsight a wonderful gift
   used wisely it will give you a boost or a lift
The age to accept whatever is there
   gently take it - always care
Impart knowledge others will gain
   but most of all fulfil all your years that remain.

C Barker

THE ALLOTMENT

Dad liked his allotment,
He liked to dig
The ground, grow
The peas and
Lettuces and
A few roses.

He often asked
Me to work on the
Allotment, no I
Did not want to,
It was his
Allotment to hoe
And see what grows,
Now he lays beneath
The seeds he sowed.

B Brown

TWILIGHT TIMES

I love it in the twilight
When the stars are half awake,
And all the air has silver hair
Around the village lake!
The sky is set with chandeliers
Which shine through thick and thin;
Then suddenly a bird is heard
And daytime songs begin!
If I ever get to heaven,
(I hope I will some day)
I wish to view from out the blue
The place I used to play!

Sharon Howells

BIRD LIFE

In the hedge Cock Robin flies to and fro
Then he stops to show off his lovely red breast,
He's a bright little fellow, and sings a sweet song -
And somewhere in that bank there's a nest,
Wood pigeons are cooing high up in a tree
And blue tits and great tits hover around
Awaiting their turn to peck at the nuts
Which I've placed high up from the ground,
The blackbirds are chasing each other about,
They come for their 'tit-bits' each morn,
And starlings, those greedy birds I cannot like
Are squabbling out there on the lawn,
In the pecking order of bird life
I think it's the sparrows hold sway,
There are always plenty of them about
Yes, each and every day,
Sometimes a few seagulls fly overhead
Or the thrush will deign to call,
The magpies are quite regular
And they lord it over all.
The swallows and swifts will come later,
And then maybe again this year
We will hear the sound of cuckoo
If it should decide to appear.
The wee Jenny Wren can be seen at times,
Or pigeons wheeling around in the air;
Yes, there's lots of bird life in the garden, -
Just make time to stand and stare.

Freda Searson

TO A SURVIVOR . . .WALK WITH ME

Looking back down through shadowy years,
Thinking why did it all have to be;
Was it your fault, do you deserve such fears?
The answer is no, but it's so hard to see;
You were alone with no place to hide,
You were locked into darkness without any key.
Had I only been with you, right by your side,
I would have said to you; child, come walk with me.

What happened is history, the truth cannot alter;
Living with the past can't be much fun,
But when you're down and seeming to falter,
Remember, I've told you, it can be done!
Turning ghosts into ancestors is the name of the game,
Live your life like it's meant to be,
Shed off your guilt, don't take the blame,
Come, walk in the sunshine, come walk with me.

Bad memories and the shadows they cast
Should be put where they rightly belong;
Firmly and squarely straight in the past,
You know in your heart you're not wrong;
But if in the cold small hours of morning,
You should wake and it's ghosts that you see,
Close your eyes and before day is dawning,
Reach out and know, you are walking with me.

John Batterham

WINTER ICE

Slowly before dawn with never a sound
Sharp and piercing frost covers the ground
Sprinkling with ivory on all that surrounds
Red berries with icing hanging so still
Crystal-tipped bracken transformed on the hill
Not green, or gold, but brittle and still
Grass that was soft and rippled in breeze
Now hard and unyielding at the base of trees
Bark turned silver in this luminous air
No leaves to be rustled, branches stripped bare
A pale sun rises bringing spectrums anew
Like millions of diamonds dancing in dew
Each berry encrusted with sparkling light
A fairytale picture after the long, cold night.

Ann Quibell

THE HOSPITAL

Not always the best of places
Yet somewhere you one day go,
Whether for an illness
Or visiting someone you know.

A nurse you will soon be meeting
Who tries to make you feel at ease,
Before you receive a doctor's greeting
To test all those and these.

On to the ward, then into bed
Seeing new faces as you tread,
Not to worry, for you will find
The people try to be so kind.
Now the routine they start,
Wires and patches to test your heart
Blood pressure gage is next on line
Will it be up or down, the comments are, that is fine.
Needles inserted into your arm
Really, no need for alarm,
Like tablets and pills
They are given to heal our ills.
As time goes by and pain is gone,
The doctors and nurses still go on
Giving their help to comfort you
Showing they care in all they do.

The day arrives when it is time to leave
Time to say thanks for the help received,
Hand-shakes, smiles as you go through the door
Hoping you don't have to return anymore.

F Burton

CIRCLE OF STONE

Have you ever happened to gaze upon a magical circle of stones
                                                  by night,
someone lurks in the shadows playing tricks on the moon's light.

Should you ever see the stones by the light of the day,
feel the power and the wisdom from so far away.

Four thousand plus years they have stood as guardians of the earth,
mother nature herself has blessed them, so priceless their worth.

Merlin himself laid the circle, African giants also laid claim,
but as midsummer dawns we all splendour the flame.

Our forefathers the Druids, paid homage the earth,
welcomed the warmth after harsh winter, a time for rebirth.

Listen to the stones as they capture the wind,
calling out loud to the gods, about how mankind hath sinned.

Go, wander through and marvel at the arches and boulders so tall,
Stonehenge, the mysterious, Neolithic stone temple is wondrous to all.

Michael Hartshorne

SAME GARDEN, ANOTHER DAY

The garden is my haven
A lovely place to be
I love it for the flowers
And sweet tranquillity.

Two cats lay languid in the early sun
Instinctively know, too much is bad for one.
When the sun is high and much too hot
Will sensibly move and find a cooler spot.

The garden is my haven
A favourite place of rest
To sit and ponder on things
Whilst I snatch a well-earned rest.

There's a Jenny Wren with babies
Ever flitting to and fro
To get them clean and nurtured
Before the sun sinks low.

The garden is my haven
A spot to work and play
There is ever a job to do in it
So, do a little each day.

A speckled hen calls most days
Struts on the mossy lawn
She chuckles here and peckles there
When satisfied goes home.

The buzzy bees are humming
Amongst the lavender beds
Satisfying their curious thirst
Around our feet and legs.

Leave well alone, there is work to be done
Before the settling of the sun
What an amazing sight to see
As they flit from flower, to shrub and tree.
They never stop 'til their work is done
Then with full heavy sacs, they buzz off home.

Yes there is a lot going on in this garden of mine
But to get in on the act all you need is the *time.*

Mariè Brown

THE DAYS OF THE TANNER AND THE FIDDLER

Do you recall the days,
When sixpence was a tanner?
A shilling was a bob,
A silver thre'pence was a fiddler,
And most miners had a job.
Half a crown was two and six,
A ten bob note was four.
A pound note was ten florins,
In shillings just a score.
Two ha'pennies for a penny,
Four farthings made the same.
Two hundred and forty pennies,
These made a pound again.
But there is something missing,
Which I will fit in neat,
Twelve pennies made a shilling,
Now the poem is complete.

Tom Grocott

OLD ANNIE

Annie was talking away her blues
as she pushed her pram full of rubbish and booze.
Nothing particular on her mind,
going nowhere, taking her time.
Stopping occasionally to check her wares,
she cheerfully ignores the constant stares.
What do they know in their sheltered lives?
What do they care if we live or die?
Annie found a doorway, down she sat,
fishing out a bottle, and an old felt cap.
'Spare a copper lady?', 'No,' she replied,
Annie sniffed and looked her in the eye.
'Bless you Miss, I'm obliged, off you go with your skin so tight,
don't know how you sleep at night.
I do not really need your dough,
thought I'd ask just for show.
For I have treasures; you have not
peace of mind, and a lot of tot.
So thank you lady, mind the steps, or
you may be sharing the pavement with the rest of us.

I D Welch

THE WORLD

The world's made
up of many
places
The world's full
with many
faces.

Many are rich with
silver and gold
Then there is poor
who have nothing
to hold.

The world's made
up of water
and land
which are fun
like sea and
sand.

Then there is
pollution
which poisons
our earth
like the sea
on which we
surf.

Can we stop this?
Can we help?
Save our ozone
layer so the
snow won't
melt.

Oh the world
what a place
with so many
problems
we have to
face.

All this because
of me and you
I can help
and so can you!

Jade Hughes (13)

LOVE

Love is faithful
Love is kind
Love is calm - and
Peace of mind.

Love forgives
Does not condemn
Love respects -
Our fellow men.

Love and hate
Go hand in hand
Love is humble
Also grand.

Love is generous
Breaks all bounds
Love is selfless
Covers all ground.

Love is needed
Love stands all
For you and me
For one and all.

Gwen Tipper

IN MEMORY OF MY BENJI

My dearest Benji, wherever I may go
I am always thinking of you and I miss you so
A walk in the woods - you loved the trees
A stroll in the evening in the warm summer breeze

I treasure the days we spent together
Forget you - impossible - I could never
I miss you so much walking by my side
In my heart dear Benji you will always abide

We were best friends you and I
I would always be near when I heard you cry
I would look after you whatever the task
Because my Benji you were true to the last

The days come and go - night-time too
And all I have left to remind me of you
Are a few souvenirs I will always save
In memory of my dear dog so good and so brave

May Ward

THE HORSE

The horse has been the servant of man, ever since time began
In Roman times Caesar's army were led, with horse-drawn chariots
                                        at their head
While in England's green and pleasant land, battles like Hastings
                                        were won or lost
Sometimes at terrible cost, with horses strewn across the battlefield
Along with the soldiers, swords and shields
The Red Indians, way out west, with flowing feathers and painted chest
On powerful stallions, bare backed did ride, the chief besplendoured,
                                        rode with pride
And Calvary soldiers, in blue and gold, kept a watchful eye
With mounted patrols, young and bold
The working horse, the heavy shire, has pulled the plough,
                                        through many a mire
And long before the age of steam, along canals the horse was seen
With coal, and timber, barges were laden, the factories to keep
                                        in motion
On race courses, across the land, beautiful horses, thoroughbreds
With graceful bodies, and lovely heads
The pride of their owner, or village squire, the jockey rides in gay attire
A silver cup to win, thrills, excitement, are at hand
And circus horses are really grand
When beautiful girls on tiptoe stand, the children gaze
With wide-eyed wonder, at such awesome splendour
In fairy tales of long ago, a prince, on a white charger came
The princess from the tower to free, locked away in captivity
In modern day, horses still play their part, alas no longer, do they
                                        pull a cart
But in London's Horse Guard parade, in glorious splendour,
                                        they may be seen
Heads bobbing, hooves trotting, they guard, Her Majesty the Queen

On summer days, down country lanes, children on ponies can be found
And in villages throughout the land, horses and riders gather
With scarlet coats, brightly shining horn, the sound of it
Brings the fox from his lair, on a lovely fresh spring morning
Yes! The horse, a servant of man has been
The most handsome of animals, ever to be seen.

Irene G Corbett

MY BOER-WAR PILGRIMAGE TO NATAL
(Thoughts on the second Anglo-Boer War 1899-1902)

I know not, why I had to come here.
'Recall, the thoughts will flow.
Just tread the path, the pressure bear,
Laud the brave and valiant souls.'

So 'trepid miles from Joburg's trap,
O'er Oliver Hoek's Nek's scenic park,
To sleepy Bergville, a tiny spot on the tourists' map.
'Thank God you reached there just before dark.'

In its sole hotel I took my rest,
Tomorrow to cross the veldt to Ladysmith.
Leaving the Drakensburgs in the mist,
There to separate facts from myth.

'Ford the Tugela and leave the Klip River to dream.
Yet another destiny to find.
Expand your purview of Buller's blunders schemed,
At the time the Empire's favoured sons died.'

Away to Colenso and Potgeiter's Drift
The same bugle-call resounds.
Cross the Tugela Heights and climb Observation Hill;
Where our boys fell with grievous wounds.

From Elandslaatge to Spion Kop they went,
Supporting and to bravely sustain,
Through storm-clouds and with patience spent
Their love of Dear Queen Victoria's Reign.

They did their best, God knows it's true.
So treading this painful path again,
With worthwhile effort, his bonus will accrue
To prove for them our love is not in vain.

Brian Harris

THE CHALLENGE

The station was outside the village
Isolated by the boggy fields,
Hidden away, as well it should
From what seemed static:
Stone with moss as facial hair, and wood,
Weathered fittingly by age alone.

The sound of space and silence filled
A need. Created tiptoe reverence,
As in a library dumb with books.
The only change: decay memorialised.
The slow but certain moulding clay
Of centuries cheered on by bells, dictated
By the crumbling churches, dreaming.

Colonel Templar-Jones lies slumbering,
United with his soil and stones,
His bones build up the village.

A rash of pebble-dash. Eyes metal frames
As council homes arise
To taunt the heavy years.
Is the village like a slumbering beast?
Are they so many alien fleas
That suck its blood and drink its tears?

Diane Burrow

PEOPLE SHOULD CARE

Did you see your sister fall, and walk
by as if nothing had happened at all?
And when your brother lay bleeding,
turn away, uncaring, unheeding?
The small child calling for your hand to lift them up,
deny even a sip from your so-full cup?
And what of the cold and hungry person sleeping in the street,
walk over them with hob-nailed boots upon your feet?
The dad who can no longer support his loved family,
as his business is now in the red,
would you kick him down, until he wishes he was dead?
Perhaps the person in pain, you would take away from the comfort
that keeps them sane?
'No!' you say to all of these, but pause for a moment if you please.
Do you care about others in everything you do?
Or is everything done by you, only for *you*?
These words I have penned to make us all aware,
how much better life would be
if only people showed love and care.

Joy R Gunstone

A Winter's Walk

Light footsteps upon the ground
Twigs that snap and make a sound,
Autumn leaves fall from the trees
Swept along by gentle breeze.

Walking by the trees so bare
Trying so hard to take care
Of our surroundings changing shape,
Till summer comes we have to wait.

The passing by of gentle feet
Pass the squirrels as they sleep,
The wind gets up, sharp as a splinter
Here comes the harsh, cruel, deep winter.

Beth Simpson (14)

GORDON AND AUDREY

G od bless you in many ways we pray
O nce on your retirement in every way,
R etire with grace as you spend your leisure hours
D o everything in love and God's wonderful powers,
O nly he can guide your life in everything you do
N ever give up the faith for not only God loves you, we do too,

A lways be receptive to his word in your life
N ow's the time to do things together with your wife
D oubts and fears leave behind also times of strife,

A gainst the devil's tricks you will still have to fight
U se all the power of God and walk in the light,
D on't forget God is with you always night and day
R emind yourselves of this each time you pray,
E veryone wishes you well in your retirement years
Y ou leave us now as we shed a few tears.

George Reed

THE MUSICAL BOX

I thought it very pretty
That box upon the side
It played a little ditty
It was my joy and pride
But fashions change so quickly
I thought it very sad
When the children thought it awful
And to keep it would be mad.
'It's surplus to requirements Mum
The bin will be emptied at noon
Stick it in there (I felt quite numb)
Along with that broken broom'
I couldn't bear to part with it
So smuggled it away
And kept it under lock and key
For a decade and a day.
Then one day came a childish voice
'Grandma, what can I do
Now my friend is away it is so dull
I want to do something new.'
So out came my surplus musical box
She seized upon it with glee -
It's got another owner now
A 'smiling' present to her from me.

Muriel I Tate

THE DANCER

No one could dance the Charleston,
Like Maudie did,
In her youth.
Her long legs would tap out
The rhythm of the music,
And the tassels on her dress
As they swung to and fro,
Almost had the crowd
In the theatre hypnotised.

They loved her,
With her black bobbed hair
Bouncing up and down.
They loved the vitality
And youthful innocence.
Maudie had them enchanted.
Now, she cannot remember those
Days of her youth.
Not anymore.

Maudie stares vacantly,
As her husband wipes away
The dribble from her mouth,
And patiently changes the urine-soaked
Stockings, for the third time that day.
She was a beauty,
He says with pride,
Until this damned Alzheimer's
Destroyed her life.

Margaret Maher

NOW SHALL WE SLEEP

Now shall we sleep,
And dream a dream,
Of visions fair,
That we have seen.

Or, will we twitch
And turn about,
A nightmare scare,
And make us shout.

Upon our pillow,
We lay our head,
When tired we all
Must go to bed.

So now we sleep,
And dream a dream:
A vision fair?
Or will we scream?

Mary McPhee

FROSTY

I've waited in for ages,
Now it's nearly half past two.
I've fed the cat and done my chores
And I'm on my seventh brew.
A telephone call I made at one
I was told that the delay
Was due to a new driver
Who didn't know his way
He'd opened up his A-Z and read it upside down
And landed in a traffic jam
On the other side of town.
So now I've wasted my whole day
And I'm getting really cross.
I had to have the day off work
And that didn't please the boss.
So hurry up please driver
It's costing me real money
My chicken's starting to smell a bit foul
And my salami's turning funny.
What's that I hear, a van at last
He's stopped outside my door
But he's delivering to the wrong address
Those lot at number four.
'Hey you,' I shout, 'It's mine you twit,' what a stupid geezer
Too late, he's gone, and my neighbours from hell, have a
                                        frost-free freezer!

Josephine Burnett

FRIENDS

Sometimes they're there
sometimes they're not
but there's one thing for sure
they won't be forgot

Sometimes you need help
and you'll have to call
they'll lend you their ear
and make you feel tall

There's no price on friendship
that is for sure
because if they need your help
they'll knock at your door

So there's one thing about friendship
that is so true
if you have a good friend
they'll be there for you

But friendship runs two ways
that's one thing I know
and if your friend calls on you
never tell them to go.

Rob Passmore

NOTHING

It's as evil as the devil
It's not even
It's not odd
All poor people have it
Though it's mightier than God

Rich folk have no need for it
It can make a mountain cry
The bravest are afraid of it
And if you eat it you will die

Maurice Ivor Birch

To The Crane-Fly

You tried so hard to keep your life,
But incensed, determined,
I sought you out, paused only
To reveal your hiding place
Where on flimsy trembling legs,
You acted out your frenzy -
Scrabbling at a picture,
Then clinging to a light,
Treadling your last vain dance,
'Til drained of life you fell and died.

Did your intricate lace of wing,
And your spindly grace of leg,
Mean nothing to me? Was your
Unceasing fervour for life,
Mine to crush and sweep away?

No, not your death grieved me,
But my desire for it,
My violence without brake
Which so much disturbed.

So to all crane-flies, welcome to
The shadows of all my rooms
And stay in peace. I've had
Enough of self-disgust.

Sylvia Anne Lees

THE VILLAGE

Oh! To be in the country now that summer's here.
Oh! To be in the country, any time of any year.
The lush green fields, you can see for miles,
The picturesque walks, with the man-made stiles.
The hedgerows and bushes, and the elegant trees
Gently swaying in the balmy breeze.

As I walk round the commons and see the ferns and heather
The bluebells and the ladysmocks I could go on forever.
To see the sheep and the cows grazing without a care
Let's hope for the next generations, they will still be there
The birds sing their songs from dawn until dark
Then next day begin singing, like the favoured lark.
When the cuckoo arrives to sing us their song
You have to listen carefully for they don't sing too long
God gave us all this nature, just for our pleasure
It's something to enjoy, and something to treasure.

Margaret Clowes
Ipstones Staffordshire Moorlands

A Touching Moment So Sublime

A moment full of blissful blend
In wintertime when hearts contend,
With youthful play and youthful screams
While valley wonder lightly gleams
And flakes of snow descend.

A soft white cloak that beautifies
The valley of the hearty cries,
So gently placed where snowdrops hide
Is pure enough for winter's bride
When whiteness purifies.

Down banks so steep the sledges race
And leave designs in snowy grace,
While silently upon the crest
Our winter's king and valley's guest
The snowman greets embrace.

Wandering winds so sharp and bold
That chase the young and freeze the old,
Form drifts of snow with playful skill
While gloveless hands ignore the chill
And scoop the snow to mould.

Enchantment of a magic scene
Enhanced by Rose a young colleen,
A touching moment so sublime
And beautiful in wintertime
When whiteness covers green.

Peter James O'Rourke

FREE

Can you honestly say, you're free?
I can, because Jesus, is with me.
He guides me on my way,
He's with me, every day.

He helps me with my poems,
He inspires me with my songs.
I always mention Him in my prayer,
Because I know He's everywhere.

Free, like the lark, in the sky,
Like all the birds that fly by.
Free, like the wind that howls along,
I feel free, when I'm singing a song.

Free, like the flowers in the meadow, that bloom,
Free as a daisy, bright, not full of gloom.
How can I tell you, that I know you're near,
You've been around, for many, many a year.

Free, like the clouds, that float up above,
Knowing you now, giving you all my love.
Jesus said, follow me, I'm the truth, the way,
Believe in me and I'll be with you every day.

Free, like the stars, that glitter every night,
Free like the moon, that shines so bright.
Knowing Jesus, that's the right thing to do,
I'll give Him my love but I'll save some for you.

William Jebb

I AM NOT AFRAID

In the deep, deepest
Darkness of the night
I am not afraid.
My Lord God is near,
I have no reason to fear.
He is close by me.

In the deep, deepest
Darkness of night
Angels watch over me.
They stand close by
Till morning is nigh.
They watch over me.

In the deep, deepest
Darkness of night
God is ever there.
If I should wake,
In His arms He'll take
Me and comfort me.

In the deep, deepest
Darkness of night
I am not afraid.

Doreen Swann

NIGHT NURSE

She is so fair
And has the flair
Night nurse is her name
And in the night she came.

Her hand on my brow
I can feel it now
Soothing and sweet
Cooling the heat.

Now I have left her care
And am back home so fair.
But I'll always remember
Those nights in December.

Sleepless nights
Giving me frights
Until she came, I feel it now
As she soothed my troubled brow.

Jack Purdom

MY FIRST BORN

You were my first born and you came late
But you were worth all the time I had to wait
As I cradled you closely to my breast -
Like a tiny bird in its mother's nest

Your hair was fair, your eyes so blue
You yawned and stretched oh! how you grew
The weeks into months and the months into years
On your first day at school I shed a few tears

Time went by fast and like the rest
You got a job and did your best
But soon you felt the need to go
Why you joined the army I'll never know

You did your time and came home to me
But not for long, it had to be
A new and interesting life
With the girl you chose to become your wife

The wedding was a grand affair
And all the family were there
I hid the pain and no one knew
Just how I felt at losing you

You were my first born I'll not forget
With my memories stored they are not with me yet
What a pity we have drifted apart
For I still love you, here in my heart

Laura Steer

TO FEEL WITHOUT YOU

Sitting here alone
the day is drawing near
no time to sleep
there's nothing to eat.

I await for your call
or a knock on the door
a smile on my face
would appear and be clear.

Thinking about my life
and how it would be
if you would appear
and make yourself clear.

To hold you tight
right by my side
would show you the love
I hold onto.

Staring into nothing
I go way beyond
the life I've got
without you.

The sadness and bitterness
that secures my heart
stops me loving another
even my own brother.

To release this pain
before I go insane
is for you to be
right next to me.

Michelle Crozier

CABBAGE PATCH

She bends over the cabbage field,
The morning fog around.
Her frizzed black curls hang with dew
She wields her surgeon's knife,
Cutting each orb of cabbage from its thickset stem.

A modern 'Tess' she works her row,
Black sweat upon her back; her orange trousers
Proof against the wanton tractor which
Relentlessly collects box upon box,
Hour by hour. These will feed the citizens of the town.

They know nothing of her toil,
The whims of sun and rain.
They drive into town in ordered line,
Read computers row by row,
Sweating under neon lights in central heating.

At five o'clock they struggle home,
Pushing through traffic as in the morn.
Exhausted, they shower, eat and watch telly.
'Tess', rested from the midday heat,
Placidly cuts another row of cabbage in the evening air.

Jane England

LADYBRIDGE
*(Written in 1996 to commemorate the finding of relics where
the old bridge stood)*

Astride the winding Anker and the thrusting Tame, stands
our bridge, the gateway to Tamworth town.
It has weathered the span of time, Saxon, Dane, Norman all have
crossed the river's line.
When first the invaders came up the Trent from the east
they found the place where two rivers met, and a settlement formed.
A fortified encampment on a mound was raised, surrounded by a
stout fence a Worth upon the Tame, the town of Tamworth was born.
Close to Watling and the Salter's was Tamworth town.
Horse, carts, and people started to wend their way into the town.
To cross the rivers which were wide was not an easy ride.
Stout piles into the river were sunk, and a wooden road was
there begun.
A stout gate at each end was built, to keep invaders out and local
people in.
The town prospered and became a mighty place.
The capital of Mercia it became where Offa built his Palace,
the Palace was the wonder of the age, and our bridge became its
landing stage.
Across its planks the soldiers of the king marched in ranks.
Merchants, peasants, lords and other kings, came to town to
give their thanks.
To Offa the mighty Saxon king who ruled and protected everything.
In time the bridge became tired, and finally it was fired.
Its flaming timbers into the Tame they fell leaving a gap
and now no more to tell.
So alas we fear to tell there was no bridge, where do we cross.
Timber though stout would not suffice, so we must seek for
new advice.

The bridge had died, the town had died.
Alas much time would pass, until the new bridge arrived.
Built of stone, longer, wider, stronger it would be
though Tamworth town then of no importance would be.

Carl Kemper

To A Rose Tree

The garden held a plot where a rose tree grew to grace,
But the garden now is mourning that sad and empty place.
She came to bring us joy in the springtime of each year
And was certain of the welcome that always met her here.
What pleasure when a branch would show a tiny curling leaf
A promise that the time was near when tender buds would peep
Then waiting for the glory as the velvet petals spread
As wafting gently in the breeze a sweet perfume was shed.
The winter came and brought the winds that blew so cold and long
And through the night the frost came down with talons cruel and strong
The battle lost and the rose tree died but she did not bloom in vain
For many shared her beauty and her memory will remain.

May Walker

BEYOND THE GARDEN WALL

What mystery and delight lies beyond the old garden wall
As the morning mist flows through the iron gates so tall
It knows no boundaries gliding amongst the old and the new
Touching webs that now sparkle with life and tremble with the dew.

Shadows of the past or is it the future fill the mind
Memories linger of the wandering souls left behind
The mist muffles the ancient church bell that rests on the hill
It rings out softly and then silent again and all is very still.

Hand in hand the warm reflection of the many blooms
Brightens up the multitude of grey stone decaying tombs
The rusty lock is heard as the gardens are open to view
Amongst the smell of thyme and fennel is coffee and Earl Grey too.

They come to view the grandeur of the Great Hall
That stands in splendour hidden behind the old brick wall
The hall gardens now await the many visitors there
In wonderment of bygone days its secrets for everyone to share.

Caroline Purser

I LOVE APPLE CRUMBLE

The steam rises slowly
curling around and around.
The mixture of sugar and marg
plus flour which is freshly ground.
Then there is the fruit that I love
from the tree that sits a silver dove.
The apples that lie
under the bed of crumble.
They are covered with sugar
and make my stomach rumble.
As I eat this delicacy
the warmth goes to my head.
From the syrup coated apples,
to the golden crumble bed.

Kate Boothroyd (12)

THE SIOUX

The Sioux sat silent astride his steed
Like a statue silhouetted against the sky
From a hill he looked down to the plains
With a look of blazing anger in his eyes

When he was sure no white men were about
He cantered down to the plains below
To survey a scene of senseless slaughter
A herd of over a hundred dead buffalo

The white men had not killed the herd for skins
Neither had they killed the herd for meat
The buffalo herd had been slaughtered
To starve the Sioux, by winter, into defeat

The Sioux cried out to the Great Spirit
The hills echoed to his piercing cry
White men had fanned the flames of war
And smoke signals spiralled into the sky

A soldier sat astride his steed
Like a statue silhouetted against the sky
From a hill he looked down to the plains
With a look of blazing anger in his eyes

When he was sure there were no Sioux in sight
Slowly he made his way down to the plain
Sickened and sad to see a scene of slaughter
Amidst smouldering remains of a wagon train

K W Benoy

TRAVEL

Ride a bike over a bridge
Take a hike over a ridge
Over the hills take a long walk
Stroll with a friend while you both talk.
Travel on a train to Scotland and back
Ride on a horse when you've cleaned all its tack.
Ride on a bus, a coach or a tram
To fetch bread, butter and blackberry jam
You can travel a long way or not very far
Use bus, coach or train or even a car.

M M Watts

LOST TIMES

People rushing - going nowhere,
No time to reflect, to stand and stare.
Like mice they scurry to and fro;
Life carries them on - and on they go.

No one has a minute to stop and chat,
They're all wrapped up in this and that.
The masses pushing to board the train;
Taking them to work and then home again.

Once at their jobs, they keep up the pace,
Each one a part of today's rat race.
Competition for jobs is now so high;
They cannot be complacent - it's do or die.

It was never like this in times gone by,
People mattered - I wonder just why
How all that has changed, it seems so sad
Community spirit; neighbourly love, once we had.

Materialism, wealth are now top of the list;
Morals and kindness rarely exist.
Greed, avarice and crime now abound
Where is love and compassion, will it ever be found?

Maggy Copeland

MILLENNIUM THOUGHT

So, the fontanelles have closed
On the Millennium Dome.
Visit if you must, be marvellously distracted,
But on your way home

Crush some herb Robert and smell
The Middle Ages, think of crude medicine,
And slight, fatalistic hope.
Run faster with the dog over the fields,
For plague has reached the next village.
Rest beneath great oaks, recall the sea,
Destiny of their growing.
Weep with parents when scarlet fever raged.
Move on a century; taste turnip pulp in jam,
Yet sweet when 'all clear' sounded.

The fontanelles have closed
On the Millennium Dome.
But a thousand years are within us all,
In song, in mirth, in loam.

Unassailable.

Jennifer McDonald

HAPPY MEMORIES

If I should die in a foreign land
When you, my dear, were not at hand,
Please grant my dying thoughts would be
Of happy times you spent with me.

Sometimes we laughed,
Sometimes we cried,
And troubles? They were put aside.
We both made plans - our future bright!
Full of hope. A shining light.

The pleasant hours - the sun-kissed days,
Our love shone through in many ways.
For you - my dear - new days will dawn,
So think of these - and do not mourn.

Les Watkins

ONE HOUR - FORWARD?

One hour forward, the clock's moved on,
Summer is here, and winter has gone!
At the end of March we lost one hour
Awoke that Sunday, found light and power.

Wise Mother Earth whispered to plants and trees
The time has come, so show yourselves please!
The spirit of new life then appeared everywhere
Showering rainbows of colour, nothing was bare.

Little lambs so white, skipped on fields so green,
This new awakening was a joy to be seen.
Warm, sunny days, were just a dream away . . .
Long hours of light now extended each day.

Then at Easter, dainty snowflakes floated from above,
Colours vanished under a white blanket of love
So silent, so still, cloaked in pure glistening white,
Unexpectedly, the season had changed overnight.

April showers then ascended, and snow vanished away,
Refreshed and colourful, nature greeted another day.
Each day is unique and changeable like us
So when it is raining use a brolly, be cheerful don't fuss!

The heavenly rain falls for us all to share
Bringing energy and life, like an answer to a prayer,
One hour *forward*, seasons change and come and go,
The weather tomorrow? Well, we just never know!

S M Bush-Payne

RELATIONSHIP RAP

Her lips are like cherries
Her face as beautiful as snow
I really, really like her
But that I think she knows
I think she's a bit shy
But I'm as confident as a bull
I think I'm in love with her
But then I love them all
I'm always writing letters
I'm always singing songs
When she gives the evil eye
I think I'm in the wrong
She likes cuddly toys
And that I understand
What really does my head in
Is when it makes a sound
Her parents really hate me
I understand why
I hope they've been abducted
And taken to the sky
When we have an argument
We fight really bad
Now we've broken up
Because I've made her sad

Gaven Clarke (14)

THE LABOURER

You can meet him every day,
Bent upon his weary way,
Chin on chest, no sign of zest,
The labourer.
All day long his weary task
He performs and never asks
No questions, nor complains he much,
The labourer.
Perhaps a little moan or groan,
He has a never-changing tone,
Happy laughter rarely greets you,
From the labourer
Gnarled hands and lagging feet,
Bitter eye, tough wind-tanned cheek,
Stooped shoulders, wearied limbs,
The labourer.
His is not to reason why,
Sweat and graft grow old and die,
Unassuming, never fuming,
The labourer.
Through the labour of his hands,
Mighty structures rise and stand,
Symbolic of his own tough frame,
The labourer.
Shouted, chaffed at all day long,
Never right but always wrong,
Bitter eye, but servile never!
The labourer.
How far would we get without him,
And his simple menial task?
We would never ask this question of
The labourer.

B Ruffles

NIL

Dream on sweet dreamer
But see the truth
Forget the innocence of thy youth.
Care for others by degrees,
For they will bring you to your knees.
Look into the mirror of life and see,
Look deep and see the one to love is thee.

So dream on dreamer and then awake,
For tomorrow it may be too late.

B George

LOST SOMEHOW, SOMEWHERE

My dearest Paul,
Why did you go?
Your father sits and sighs,
We both love you so,
Our heads hang in grief,
Perhaps we were too severe,
Not kind enough perhaps,
Or was it a mere
Misunderstanding.
Come back, God knows we love you,
Make us happy, then perhaps,
We will accept your point of view,
You will come back, please!

But Paul did not appear,
That chilly spring day,
Or the following year,
His mother's face he never saw again.
The telegram never did arrive,
It said plainly, killed in action,
From what I could derive,
It was lost somehow, somewhere
And I not born,
When this event occurred,
Was on some distant morn,
I, was destined to find it!

Alan Dawes

SHALL WE DANCE

The kids flew the nest, they have long since gone.
Now I'm a widow, all alone
Life is not over yet, d'you want to bet?
I never could stand folks who moan
So if you think that I'm finished
Then think it no more
For come eight o'clock I am out of the door
I whoop it up nightly
With pensioners sprightly -
No one to tell me to stop
Though my chest has a wheeze
I've screws in my knees
I can still do a jive and a bop
It is never too late to try something new
You are never too old to learn
So put best foot forward whatever you do
Just side step and chassis and turn.

Olive Allgood

LIGHT-HEARTED.LOOK@LOVE

To: icu_iwantu@loveme.com
From: loveme_notmyface@misfit.com

Love between two people
Is it possible?

Eternal,
Till death do us.
I mean, c'mon, seriously, love?

Hollywood Romances
Willis and Moore and strippingandAggassiandtennis
andshieldsand Robertsandoldmen
andmoney . . .

No . . .
Love between two people *is not* possible.

We love so many in one lifetime,
From Tony-with-the-cute-dimples to Brad-with-the-rich-dad.
We fall in, we fall out
Halfway there (distracted by new-guy-with-no-name, to find it is
Wilmott, then back to the mission at hand).

Love
A computer screen flickering on and off.
Like you and me
Sharing this moment
Virtual chat via the web.
Nothing but words.

Meanwhile,
The true, loyal, lifetime companions hide behind the
                                not-so-perfect face.
The misfits,
The problem-page writers.
The protoforms of the plastic people in magazines.

Love between two people *is* possible.
Look past the surface,
Go down into the tunnel and there at the bottom
You'll find a secret door and if you're lucky,
You'll have the key to it.

I'm still looking for mine.

N B Dahl

CHERUB TARGET MISS

My angel wings are broken,
My fairy dust blown away,
My cherub song is silent
And my childhood here to stay.
Smothered by my innocence,
Intoxicated when I'm near,
Loved for eternity
Would bring about your fear.
Inebriated on your words,
High on your smile,
Emotion of increasing amplitude
Would suffer from your denial.
You fled from my commitment,
Asphyxiated by my need,
And severed all my longings
For you could not fulfil my greed.
Now my wings are torn and tattered,
And my dust has lost its wish,
And cherub forgot the tune
When his arrow and your heart did miss.

Hayley Beddoes

SENTIMENTS OF A BLIND PERSON

I hear the click of the garden gate,
I feel the warmth of the sun on my face,
I hear the laughter of children at play,
I hear the song of the birds so gay,
I hear the bark of the dogs at night,
I can only sense the moon so bright
For my eyes are sightless.
I cannot see, blind from birth,
Is how God made me.

I still can find much happiness
For as I walk through the park,
Though I am sightless, I still can feel
That feeling of pleasure upon me steal,
As I meet a friend, who's voice I know,
I stop for a chat, and as the cool winds blow
I can smell the perfume of the roses sweet,
I can smell the dust of the dusty street,
What have I missed, so much yet so little.

So much in life, has passed me by,
I often hear other folk sigh
When I'm down-hearted and I need to cry
I count my blessings, and think of the joy.
I can give to others, as life goes by,
For God in his wisdom has given to me
So many blessings, that I am free
From the sight of sorrow and the sight of pain
That in my wisdom I have so much to gain.

D A Hampton

RAINBOW THROUGH THE RAIN

I've given you a path to take
you must walk this path alone,
but have no fear,
have no doubts
I will not leave you on your own.
Listen for my footsteps
as I follow on behind.
And listen for my voice, soft and ever kind.
Just like a faithful shepherd,
I will not leave my lamb,
so walk the path that I have shown,
where you are,
So am I.
Just as the father loves his child,
so I my child love you,
so trust in me
have faith in me,
and I will bring you through.

And when this path you leave behind,
you are back, from whence you came.
Then my child,
once more you'll see
the rainbow through the rain.

Jacqueline Claire Davies

VAMP

Down in a cavern, where the sun never shines,
There's creepy crawlies, clinging to vines.
Down in a cavern where it's cold and damp,
Lives a terrible creature, whose name is Vamp.
Down in a cavern where I'd never go,
Vamp screams and howls, why? I don't know.
Down in a cavern sounds horrid to me,
So I'll stay home and have worms for tea.

Sue Knight

ARMY TRAINING

Every morning I awake and think,
I could be home having a drink,
With my mates down the town,
But still, I'm here, with constant frown.
I have new friends Smith and Lee,
But I wish my family were here with me.
For myself, I fight this fight,
I'll get through, but it might be tight.
Four more weeks and I'll be home,
To have a drink and probably moan.
Two days off, then I'll be back,
To fight for Queen, and clean my tack,
Some more hard work then I will find,
Myself at Windsor or behind enemy line.
Passing out I'll soon be,
With my family watching over me.
I'll soon be home, leave is due,
Sitting and talking just with you.

Jon Knight

ANTITHESIS

I am the blade that will not be sharpened
I am the wheel that will not turn
I am the dark that will not lighten
I am the flame that will not burn
I am the emptiness
I am the void
I am the one who sits beside
The whore of Babylon
Hear my laughter
As I spit seeds of destruction
I am the horned one
I am the one that all men fear
I am the one that all men desire
I am the one that all men devour
From nothing to nothing
For nothing
Is my clarion call
Belief is deceit
Worship, a fallacy
I am the bloated
Wanton child
Of an imbecilic race
And I am undeniable.

Ian Davies

INDIAN BRAVE

Indian Brave stands
Atop a sun-dried mountain
Snake eyes survey the scene,
Below, is this happening?
Nightmare, more than dream,
Below, shouting, yelling, crying,
Screaming of the guns,
Arrows flying, hitting men,
Hitting brass upon the blue
Men dying, blood everywhere,
Horses whinnying, bite the dust,
Brave eyes staring empty to the sky.
A pole grasped by blood-red hand,
Warrior Brave's running, hold gun high,
Away from Custer's last stand.

J Neville

SWAN WOMAN

I saw a swan,
a swan woman,
an untamed beauty,
on a turquoise lake.
Magical union.
A winged, white sacrifice,
like a heart-white woman
on water bright.
Passionate nature of beauty,
against hail-stoned fury,
on sometimes turbulent waters.
Love me!
Please enter my sanctuary!

Paul Darby

MY POOR OLD TEETH

Oh! I wish I'd looked after me teef,
Me dentist bill beggars belief,
For me toothache was giving me grief,
So a visit I paid for relief.

As I sat in the dentist chair,
And uttered a silent prayer,
He said, 'You should've taken more care,
For the enamel on your teeth, it's laid bare.

Next he said he would have to do some filling,
He dug here and there, then he started drilling,
For the holes and the cracks were just like craters,
And as soft in parts as mashed potatoes.

Now! The sweets I had eaten seemed much less attractive,
As the dentist's drill was just far too active,
And as the noise of pulled teeth fell into his dish,
How I wish I'd eaten more apples and fish.

Now the teeth I have left, I'll treasure like gold,
Then maybe they'll last me until I get old,
And I'll brush them religiously, both morning and night,
And I'll treasure me peggies and all food that I bite.

B G Taylor

OCEAN

Calm blue ocean,
Slowly lapping at the shore,
Housing all the wonderful creatures,
And me all alone, swimming in peace,
The wonders of the ocean are clear to me now.

Robert Wood (10)

YOUR FEELINGS DO MATTER

The deepest and the darkest
Hidden out of sight.
Throughout the painful day,
And never-ending night.

Comfort rarely visiting,
Soon to be replaced.
By the fear and the betrayal
Of the human race.

Talk to me, write down your fears
Pen and paper can't judge or abuse.
Slowly uncoil the pain within,
You really have nothing to lose.

There are souls trusted to listen
Don't despair on your own anymore.
Don't be ashamed of what is inside,
Hunt it out, to the very core.

I'm telling you, your feelings do matter
In your darkest hole, there is someone to care.
The road to inner peace,
May never cease.
But at least you can start the repair.

Sheila Sarson

FASHIONS

Here I sit watching people pass by
Most are clad to catch the eye
Is that a man with hair of gold?
No! It's a smart suited lady, so I'm told.

A pair of teenagers, arms entwining
Baggy tops and shorts are what they're wearing
Happy in their expectations
The togs they wear are for relaxation.

An elegant creature with long flowing hair
With beautiful dress, worn with a flair.
Many eyes and whistles follow her
She's pleased but pretends not to hear.

Were I to dress as one of these
With flowing hair or shorts to my knees
Many eyes with glee would follow me
Because you see, I am *ninety-three.*

Gwynneth Daley

SNOWDONIA MORNING

The cracking echoes to scissor blackbirds,
Chinks and grykes clatter as
Warm water wells under the pane frost,
Left after Epiphany's last gasp.

Peak-shadows swing and lengthen. Ashlars,
Sunk in the basalt-black, sway
Under the static, windless, billion watt
Torch over parsley-white biochemistry.

Wicker reeds as stilites in the ice:
Press-ganged sundials gather as
Warm water thaws their mossy meridians
Over micro cotyledon pasts.

Ex cottages, now built of bone, breathe,
Exhaling millilitres of hair
Into freezing, sunscreened, bearded mouths,
Excavating, metal-detecting the air.

Milky crystals leak blue. Sulphate
Of copper into the lakes below
The reflected Urubamba's greenish peak,
Twelve hours behind Eryri's glow.

A J Strange

TRUE LOVE

You are my sunshine, you are my light
Always beside me by day and by night
My love for you is never in doubt
You are my light that will never go out.

You're in my thoughts always
Deep down in my heart
How sad I am feeling
When we are apart.

Soon we'll be married
Together we'll stay
So happy united on our wedding day,
Sharing our problems as they arise
And trust in each other
So our love never dies
Good times and bad times
Together we will share
Then love for each other
Will always be there.

Bob Reynolds

ALIVE AND KICKING

Life begins when you are born,
A small but noisy little form,
Huddled to your mother's breast
In a nappy and warm vest.

You slowly grow, and with your dummy,
Stop the pain of teeth through gummy,
You then progress to solid food,
And just don't *care* about being nude.

Next to nursery school, that's right,
Where maybe *learn* to read and write,
For companionship and all its joys,
Sharing other children's toys.

Onward then to primary school,
Pencils, pens and a one foot rule,
A blazer - tie of school design,
The report that says you're doing fine.

On to high school, college too,
Working out what you want to do,
Tradesman - doctor - computer stuff,
Remember training can be awful tough.

You finally leave and find a job,
Or you become a bloody yob,
Of course by now, you've read the text,
And know all about the opposite sex.

Now is the best time you have had,
And think your mum and dad are sad,
But just remember, you're just part way,
Will you of the distance stay.

John Bright

L IS FOR LONELINESS

L is for loneliness, solitary and sad
O is for outcast, it makes you feel bad
N is for nobody, your importance feels slight
E is for enemy, the world is not nice
L is for listen but your voice is not heard
I is for isolate, participation deferred
N is for never, to be included in life
E is for equivalent, but you always lack fight
S is for society, which does not with you share
S is for silence, when you are no longer there
     unable to cope with a life of despair.

Jan Le Bihan Panter

THE NEW MILLENNIUM

That magical night on New Year's Eve,
With those magical millennium keys,
That the door to the year 2000 was opened,
Kept back with rope and string.
All those hopes and dreams and wishes
The new millennium could bring.
From the year behind are thousands of memories,
Some blown away with a millennium breeze.
So look over the hills and out in the distance
Down to a sparkling sunrise.
Out there behind that magic,
The new millennium lies.

Philippa Chalmers (10)

THE JOURNEY TO SUMMER

With Christmas delight far gone by
The New Year passed and springtime nigh
I dream of days in golden sun
Roses in bloom, the spider's web spun
When I shan't feel the presence of time
And all the world is truly divine
To be free from this land
And to drift through the sky
Like a feather dancing to a sweet lullaby
Somewhere I will find a magical place
Where the blossom falls, where the unicorn race
Fairies flutter their sparkling wings
And at the water the mermaid sings
The elf and the pixie, a celebration of love
And overhead swoop a pair of white doves
This place is called summer
And summer is enchantment
On the journey there happiness is ever-present
Beside me holding my hand you fly -
The pair of white doves
That are you and I.

Ali Dodds

THE BROKEN HEART

How do you mend a badly broken heart?
Which prescription do you choose
When the organ so sadly riven apart
Won't respond to any treatment that you use?
How do you mend a heart that lies in pieces?
What mode of action do you take
When the sorrow that caused this steadily increases
Overwhelming every effort that you make?

Transplants seem strangely lacking in success
When this kind of breakage appears;
By-passing this one won't cure the distress
When the owner is constantly in tears
For the loss of a heart lying shattered and yet
That beats on in the hope of a cure;
That ever remembers, that cannot forget
A love it believed would endure.

How do you heal another fractured heart
When thousands are strewn around the globe?
With such an epidemic where do you start?
As a surgeon, where would you probe?
This is one case it's impossible to handle -
Beyond the call of duty it would seem -
Unless you can kneel and, with a votive candle,
Send a prayer to resuscitate a dream.

Dorothy Thompson

TIME

In the sunset of our lives,
And nestling out of sight
Are the happiest years of all, they say,
But I wonder if they're right?

The pride in small achievements,
But with feelings of regret
That things might have been much better -
This I simply must forget.

There should be time for leisure,
Exploring different climes,
Things to enjoy, without remorse,
But will there still be time?

There's too much time for thinking
Of things that might have been,
Instead of giving heartful thanks
For fulfilment of our dreams.

This needs a happy ending,
But of this there is no doubt,
No more procrastination
For time could be running out.

Joan Mathers

WHAT IS IT?

I bet you'll never guess
What I have seen today,
It really made me chuckle,
Blew all my cares away.

It started about seven,
Went on till noon at least,
Soon as I knew what 'it' was,
I stood and watched the beast.

What a difference 'it' made,
To cars and lorries all,
As 'it' stood there so silent,
The men inside seemed small.

Not a sound came from 'it',
As four beady eyes looked out,
Drivers eased from fast to slow,
In case 'it' gave a shout.

When a policeman came up,
Those drivers began to quake,
Lower in their seats they shrunk,
Their cars all seemed to shake.

When the clocks said twelve noon,
'It' up and trundled away,
And that's the last we saw, of
The recent traffic survey.

Isobel Crumley

DEWDROPS

A dewdrop on a petal falls
After rain has left its mark
The sun then brings its coloured rays
Until the skies grow dark

The colours are of rainbow hues
Oh! What a sight to see
Another of His wonders
Put here for you and me

There's red, yellow, pink and blue
Orange, purple and green
All these colours enrich our world
Creating every scene

Mary Aris

MOTOR RACING BOYS

I'm fed up with little squirty boys
Who drive around and make big noise
What is it with these guys roaring round
Just near to death I'll be bound.
I've gone a second more than you,
That will set your hat askew

How faster than fast can these guys go?
All the petrol, all the strife, then
Someone goes and loses life
Is it worth it just to say *I* went
Half a second faster than you today

I'll squirt you, you squirt me!
I'm fed up with squirty champagne
Boys, who race around and make
Big noise.

Laura Moore

SHEFFORD

I wish I lived in Shefford
many years ago,
and watched the barge go to the wharf,
by which a horse did toe.

To see the windmill in its field
grinding up the corn,
and now it sits there all alone
looking so forlorn.

The steam trains whistled into town
going off to Bedford,
the bridge is down, the tracks have gone
that once led it to Shefford.

There used to be a market
that went all down the street,
where women and small children
would go with friends to meet.

There used to be the fields of crops,
of corn and veg they grew,
but now the fields are full of houses
all of them brand new.

Liz Osborne

YOUR FATE

One day old Dr Death may pay a call on you
to tell you that your time is through
on this earth anyway.

He'll say, 'Ah brother, try not to be late
or you'll miss St Peter at those pearly gates
though, on the other hand maybe not.

But either way it's your time to go
up or down, even I won't know
you see, to me it's just another job.'

A J Marshall

THE DAY THE MAGPIES CAME

On seeing a framed photograph
On a stall at Newton Abbot Market

It was a happy garden scene.
How could you then have known
The numbered job-lot into which
Your likeness would be thrown!

They might have given you burial.
They might have spared you shame.
They might have done a dozen things,
The day the magpies came.

But when they'd picked and pecked about
This was your resting place.
The magpies came and took your gold,
But left your smiling face.

And now a stranger honours you,
And renders homage due,
And prays that you have gained your goal
In fit surroundings new.

Perhaps your smile illuminates
Another kind of sphere,
Where magpies cannot desecrate
Another's smile or tear.

Olive Summerfield

TRAY-CUSHION THOUGHTS

I brought me a tray, with a cushion attached,
To eat my TV meals on
But what do you think, I felt attacked,
By the bug of writing on.

To pen my thoughts to all who read
Poems from far and wide.
I feel there is a bond, a seed,
To keep us side by side.

Together we write, our thoughts, our hopes.
Exchange our views, to share.
To the web of words we all elope
From the pages we listen and hear.

Voices of hope, telling their tale,
Of things in life they fear.
Riding the storm, winds and gale,
Conquering, because they dare.

Life is to live, enjoy its pleasures,
To plan it's time to enjoy it all.
Time for work and for leisures,
That way, we can all have a ball.

Don't worry what other people have
Just look inside for your own gift.
Ask yourself, what it is you gave,
To your day to give one other a lift.

Back to my cushion with tray upon,
I rest my case where it all began
With cup of coffee, also bourbon
A poem I wrote, I'm sure we all can.

Love to you all, wherever you are
All you who stop, and stand and care.

June Chorlton

REBECCA

She remembers me, by only in the absence of my touch,
I remember her, but only when I falter at the edge of sleep.
She feels me, but only when her lips leave mine own,
I feel her, but only when she sleeps in my arms.
She misses me, but only when I stray from her eyes,
I miss her, but only when my heart beats.

David Glyn Williams

UNDETERRED

One November Sunday evening,
Thin carpets of unexpected snow
Lingered on little lawns.

Warm in their small chapel,
A depleted congregation
Awaited the first hymn:

'All hail the power of Jesu's Name!'

The organist launched 'Diadem',
Unsung for years, but seven
Keen voices - bass and unison -
Ensured it hammered Heaven!

Later that evening,
On the radio,
A balanced, polished choir,
Presenting a programme of hymns,
Sounded lovely but lacking!

Dora Hawkins

YOUNG LOVE

Her tears streamed down and splashed upon the note
Mingling all the words she'd often heard him quote
Tender words so believable, so meaningful, ones she held so dear
Breathless times he'd held her close and whispered in her ear
How could he treat her in this dreadful way
When once he'd sworn his love, until his dying day
Oh fickle, callous youth, nothing's as it seems
Breaking girlish hearts and her foolish dreams

G G Swepstone

WILLOW

Willow is a songthrush
A speckled-chested bird
And when his beak is opened
No sweeter song I've heard

Willow is a songthrush
He likes to eat the grubs
That live around our garden
In the bushes and the shrubs

Willow is the songthrush
His favourite food is snails
You can see him trying to find them
By following their trails

Willow is a songthrush
And now dark nights are here
We do not see so much of him
'Til spring arrives next year

Sandra Gibson

SUMMER

On a warm, balmy August day
I sit and watch the roses sway
Their pretty heads heavy with dew
And petals reaching out
To the sky of blue
Bees hum their gentle song
While the grass grows green, lush and strong.
A soft breeze blows in the air
And here I sit without a care
For here I am in the midst of a summer's day
Watching nature pass my way
Don't blink your eye
For you might miss
It's colourful splendour, sweet as a kiss
Butterflies flit between sunlight rays
Making the most of summer days
The garden is a blaze of brilliant hue
That God has given, just for you.

Julie Asbury

AN EVER-CHANGING LANDSCAPE

Today, waking is the dawn chorus
And drawing back the curtains to a
Boundless vista of verdant pasture.
An old tree of sev'nty years and plus!
Still gathers nurture from the earth as indeed it must.

Humble ragged hedges fringe each field.
Whilst yonder on the far horizon
Borders of a different gender.
Where urban suburbia combine.
Nothing to worry about at this moment in time.

As sunset falls and shadows lengthen
Soon the pastorial image fading
Yields to the mystery of darkness.
Whilst a neon pageantry of light
From the outer precincts provides a wondrous sight.

Dawn breaks across the sleepy land.
A white blanket of glistening snow
Untrodden and perfect covers all.
The morning mist is the skyline drape.
As I gaze out over the ever-changing landscape.

A young man from the planning office
Replete with briefcase turns up one day.
Surveys our panoramic setting.
A thousand homes, business park as well
And what is more he muses, the owner wants to sell!

P M Hanson

THE STATUE

He stopped to admire
The most perfect maiden.
Touched her,
His hands reaching those
Curves and crevices.
Now, looking at her visual
Expression,
If only she was real.
He turned away,
The life-size bronze maiden
Appeared from behind her image.
She, too had the same thoughts,
Her perfect man disappeared.
Could two perfect beings
Fall in love,
Or just admire one another
In the garden of Eden?

Mavis Smith

PMT

Well it's that time of month again
Just look at me, that's right you've guessed it's PMT
Look at my face, I look ten years older,
With dark circled eyes and a stomach like bolder.
I feel just like a Jekyll and Hyde,
One word from you and I snap inside.
I don't want to be so horrible and mean,
But deep down inside I just want to scream.
Never mind, I know it will pass,
The things you put up with because you're a lass!

Jayne Rose

A Dormouse

When the first blush of autumn touches blackberry leaves
And, berries, will varnished by the sun
Show for all to feed,
The dormouse comes
Appears, and, leisurely, with all decorum
Attends to his once depleted, now extending, tum

When the last of the red and brown, wind-tired leaves
Touch the ground
The dormouse goes
Taking with him summer
And autumn's larder

As winter days like winter days
Can wet, cold, dry-crack be
The very last cling on tenacious leaf
Touches its awaiting comrades
To try a leaven warmth in the deepest
Grooven hollows of old oak roots
Wherein a little deeper beneath
Last year's fallen leaves, lies the dormouse
With not a blackberry, nor a bill on his mind

Andy McMaster

HARVEST TIME

It was autumn
Harvest time
And there she was
Round and ripe and firm
Ready to gather him in
To harvest him
As she had
For many a lad
Before
As Laurie Lee said
There was always a Rosie
So he did his best
To help her divest
Him of his virginity
Not that she needed much help
And he would never forget that day
In the hay
And his gratitude to her
For having been there
For him then
When he needed her

W B McDade

A DAYTIME NIGHTMARE

By bus and tube and train I go
The morning rush it is so slow,
People run to stand in line
So they can get to work on time.

The weather it is cold and wet,
A daily paper I must get,
Will it always be the same
Must I play the waiting game.

Rushing, pushing all the way
Repeat it all at the end of the day,
It is real this life of mine
Just to get back home in time.

But if in a city you reside,
You'll understand this suicide,
Be it day or be it night
It's up at dawn to repeat the fight.

Come Sunday, I will stay in bed,
Relax maybe, in the garden shed,
For Monday morning comes too soon,
And again I dance to the fiddler's tune.

Loraine Richmond

THE PIANO LESSON

C, D, E, F, G,
Why is it such a mystery to me,
I'm climbing up the wall, while climbing up the scale,
My fingers are all thumbs, and now I've broke a nail.

Sharps and flats, a crotchet then a quaver,
Is it any wonder that I stop and waver,
Right hand plays the treble, left hand plays the bass,
By the time I've finished this, I'll be a mental case.

Some notes are on the lines, and some are in the spaces,
My teacher says it's simple as she puts me through my paces,
The staves are black with notes, I really am appalled,
I think across this page a spider must have crawled.

It's sounding better now, I'm getting there I think,
Yes, yes, I'm trembling on the brink,
Teacher's standing there, looking all aghast,
'My word,' she cries, 'you've played a tune at last!'

Pauline Wilkins

To Live Again

The man awoke, he had slept long and well,
yet, before the sleep, he had visited and returned from Hell.
His ordeal now over, he desired to live again,
a fresh beat pulsed through every vein.
The dark waves of doom gone, as the storm died,
replaced with gentle ripples on the turning of his tide.
He had stood for what he perceived as right,
against the majority and its unjust might.
He made mistakes and lost fickle friends,
and learnt what some men do, to justify their ends.
He had clung to straws by the light of day
at night, his mental torture never went away.
Though he was beat, it was not enough,
they stripped him of his pride, marked his dignity as rough.
Yet, with life's pillars washed away,
he somehow held on, with the passing of each day.
Then yesterday at last, the truth prevailed,
too late for some, his vessel of forgiveness, had sailed.
Though vengeance is not what he sought,
nor malice in his heart there caught.
The man was awake, he had slept long and well,
such sleep denied this past two years, inside a prison cell.

Phil Aylward

CARNOUSTIE 99

The Scottish Open no one could have expected the turn.
Such a tournament upset by the Barry Burn.
Top golf players old and new.
Tested their skills, as they knew what to do.
Day after day surprises occurred.
No one could believe the penalties incurred.
The greens were the finest, there was no doubt.
They certainly weeded the better players out.
Luck I admit did play a part.
Some appeared more honoured from the very start.
Jean Van de Velde led to the very last hole.
The clubhouse in sight, the claret jug his goal.
Chances missed and shots took in haste.
He was lucky to get a play-off place.
Justin Leonard and Paul Lawrie were also given a chance.
Rain poured down as the three took their stance.
At the end of the four holes, a champ there would be.
There was certain no favourite after the first tee.
Slowly Lawrie took the lead.
The eighteenth in sight, would he succeed?
From the eighteenth tee Lawrie was the best.
He had the shots and he stood the test.
First on the green, it all looked good.
The other two chasing, doing the best they could.
Everyone so proud how Scotsman Lawrie had done.
He holed his shot, the championship won.
A local man had won the prize.
He did play well, but it was a surprise.

Anne Sackey

THE PRINCE OF SLEEP

I saw, at last, the prince of sleep,
His was a still, but lovely face,
And in the veil of troubled night,
He touched my brow with fingers light.

That, eased my cares and showed my woe,
His fragility gave me courage,
Obliterated every fear,
I tried to speak - he did not hear.

The longed-for slumber did overtake,
And answered, was my prayer,
I know he wandered through a valley steep,
Silently, no time to spare.

In my dreams I whispered
To that lonely place - return
Dear prince return again,
To touch my tearful face.

Beryl Holroyd-Fidler

THE ROBIN

Outside it is winter with snow on the ground,
And the wind is howling all around.
On the tree branches Jack Frost leaves his mark,
Tracing his patterns onto the bark.
A robin is pecking down on the ground,
Enjoying the titbits that he's just found.
With his ruffled feathers and breast so red,
He is sitting there waiting just to be fed.
I'll throw out some crumbs and back he will fly,
Under the trees where the snows lie.
When winter has gone you can hear him sing,
He'll be building his nest because it's spring.

Alice Stapleton

THE STORM CHILD

The wind was howling wild outside
And in her arms a tender child
With cheeks as pink as a summer flower
And eyes as crisp as an April shower
All wrapped in white so sweet and pure
Her gentle eyes became unsure
A sparkle flickered in her eyes
As thunder rolled across the skies
And lightning hit the window pane
Then all went quiet once again
The storm was over, the rain had gone
And in the room a new light shone
The gentle cries of a newborn life
Cut the silence like a knife
And uncontrolled her hands they shook
As in her arms her child she took
She felt her heartbeat deep within
And touched her almost silky skin
There are no words that could describe
The feelings that she felt inside
The sweat and pain was all worthwhile
Just to see her tiny smile
A precious moment in her heart
A brand-new life, a brand-new start

Joanne England

DUET

Gravely, but with courtesy
We two tread out a star dance round each other
In orbits which may not be broken.
Too close, should even fingers touch, would be to burn
Blazing in aspects of the sun at noon
With incandescent glory.

Yet how much more to be desired than the relentless, slow
Numb ache of separation
Drifting, alone and unfulfilled.

Therefore with pace and dalliance we,
Having no more than all to lose
Pass and repass
Shaping with care the movements of our mutuality.
And looking back on where our feet have trod
Observe that in our courtesy abides the grace of God.

Diana R Cockrill

THE MERMAID

Her smile was gentle to behold
Such sweet red lips could never scold
Or so the sailor's story told
Down beneath the sea.

Her hair was long and golden too,
Her breasts were firm and in full view,
Her eyes were so very blue,
Down beneath the sea.

She made her home among the reefs
And sang her song of watery deeps
Of how the ocean takes and keeps
Down beneath the sea.

The lookout was the first to see
This beauty rise from out the sea
And like a man dived gallantly
Down beneath the sea.

His ship sped onward into shoals,
Her bow was torn with gaping holes
So perished eighty honest souls
Down beneath the sea.

R G Stevens

THE TEA ROOM

A wooden door I enter in
Oh to my delight
Into another time
Which is so out of sight.

Hot buns and tea
Content is me
For only a short time
The china bell that I ring to say 'I'll order just now.'

A lovely smile
A warmth within
From people close by
I stand up and say 'Goodbye.'

The tea room is a special place
I hope I see it soon
As this is my delight
I've gone into another time which is so out of sight.

Heather Creighton

MEMORIES

Why do memories from the past
Long buried and assumed we have seen the last
Arise as if from the grave
Our present quiet to plague
In mischief spirit form to haunt
Our thoughtful endeavours to taunt
And in process to cast a spell
To imbalance the thoughts upon which we dwell
They stem from common source
Well nurtured from the seed of remorse
As if from some weed, seed sown
We play the gardener's role to disown
If in this belief we believe
We are in thought deceived
If this canker is to be destroyed
Future noble deed and thought are alloyed.

B Norman

FOUR-WHEELED WORDS

There is murder in the driver's eyes. I have cut him up badly,
he is mouthing words: obscenities. I let him chase me, gladly . . .

I must be driving you crazy, seat-belted and lazy. My senses are all
hazy. The comfort I am feeling - *smash* - crushed, mangled, bleeding.

'Love it fast, three points for speeding - a team of paramedics needed.'

As luck had it I was mended. I have no anger: no malice intended.

I need to take the road again: to speed again, the sharpest of bends.
Forget my family and friends.

Not far of junctions, doing sixty, in a car so fast and sharp and nifty, in
a thirty zone I'm slow at fifty. The kids who see me pass all love me . . .

I used to love the look of clothes, they would fit like skin - like being
on shows. Parading clubs and pubs, abodes, where I looked good, but:
no one else could. Well, they should. Like me.

Well now my jacket is a blood-red Fiesta, with black shady windows -
I like nothing but the best. Oh, you may call me vain, but it passes the
test. I'm the coolest of drivers . . . but I mess people's lives up.

The coolest boy cruising, there's no way I'm losing. I will race any car:
I would beat them by far.

I'm the coolest one here in the car park. It's where we hang out,
it's what life's all about.

A girl and my friend in the back of the car, they tell me to floor it,
but I'm the one in charge.

But I can show them the thrills, and we speed on some pills, yeah:
some people get killed, but *we* won't. We're too young, and we're
just having fun. I wink at the girl in the rear-view mirror,
I laugh at her, we hit a tree and I kill her . . .

Simon Waters

THIS ISLAND EARTH

There's nothing more British than a forest of oaks,
Like Constable's landscapes,
Or Churchill's quotes,
In serene Scottish highlands such scenery evokes
The all stirring sound of Elgar's notes.

There's nothing so quaint as afternoon teas,
With polite village cricket,
Or fresh strawberries,
By an 'Epsom Derby' or coastal sea breeze,
This enviable island to far countries.

There's nothing more sovereign than a wild English rose
By the romance of 'Shelley',
Or the Lord Byron's prose,
From a Shakespeare sonnet those elements enclose
The majestic beauty this language bestows.

There's nothing so venerable as patriotic Scribes
From the humble sincerity,
This nation so prides
In a land of dialects each county divides
This remarkable realm such poetry imbibes.

There's nothing reassuring like sweet April rain
Or a gold summer meadow,
Or a cold winter's wane,
Nor the valleys of 'Rhondda' when spring's in flame
This proud sceptred isle of lion's mane.

There's nothing this island no ill should befall
From the strength of its children,
With backs to the wall,
United as one to defend evermore,
Eternal Britannia, mother of all.

Michael Gardner

Seaside

The best days of my life have been beside the sea,
The closest place to heaven is what it holds for me,
The freedom and the sunshine, the sand between your toes,
The bracing salty breeze, as through your hair it blows.

To explore amongst rock pools, warmed by the sun,
Run down to the sea, kick and splash and have some fun,
Past the tumbling waves, watch the boats on the sea,
Stretch your eyes to horizons, wonder where they may be.

The lovers take their stroll as day gives way to night,
Where worries soak away, where everything seems so right,
Absorb the power of the sea, the most powerful on earth,
And reconsider your position, no matter what you are worth.

Show your children the wonder, put the nature into their hands,
Collecting shells, dig some holes, make castles in the sand,
Tell them just how feeble the human race can be,
For all our power, our wisdom, we are no match for the sea.

When your holiday is over, gone for another year,
To leave the seaside, her magnetism, shed a silent tear,
Back to work, normality, the winter, cold and rain,
And count the days'til your holiday, beside the sea again.

David Whitehouse

SCOTLAND

This land of many mountains, secluded lochs and moors
This land where the magnificent golden eagle soars
This land where the Loch Ness Monster is a mystery
Scotland this place so steeped in ancient history

This land where bluebells and purple heather grows
This land where the crystal clear winding river flows
This land with its rugged mountains towering so high
Scotland this place where elusive fish eating ospreys fly

This land where dense pine forest profusely grows
This land where the mighty river Clyde ebbs and flows
This land with such beautiful scenery second to none
Scotland this place where herds of wild deer freely run

This land where people are a nation proud and strong
This land where by my birthright I live and truly belong
This land where I grew up and where I married my loving wife
Scotland this place where I hope to spend the rest of my life

Anthony Carlin

LIFE

We are only stardust,
Lighting up the dark,
We've come a real long way,
Since Noah built his ark,
But what have we really done,
We don't seem any happier,
From when God sent his son,
We're all here together,
On this spinning earth,
So why can't we ever,
See what life is worth,
Through each generation,
We stager blindly on,
We won't know what we had
Till everything is gone.

June V Johnson

THE LORD IS MY KEEPER

T ulips
H eathers
E chinops

L ythrums
O rchids
R oses
D affodils

I rises
S alvias

M arigolds
Y uccas flaccids

K ochias
E vening primrose
E chions
P ansies
E rodiums
R omneyas

All these flowers were once laughter,
That fell upon the earth.
For all the angels danced and sang,
When God gave man his birth.

M Murphy

AND IF . . .

And if the day should ever dawn
   when I awake and find you gone
No more your smile, your lovely face
No more your laughter, your embrace
   I could not carry on . . .

And if the day should ever dawn
   when you no longer share my night
No more your scent, your breathing deep
My arms around you as you sleep
   Then nothing would be right . . .

And if the day should ever dawn
   when it's time for one of us to go
I'll keep you safe within my heart
For the time we have to be apart
   Because I love you so . . .

And if the day should ever dawn
   when we know we have to say goodbye
No more to feel your kiss, your touch
Or be held by the man I love so much
   I know that I would die . . .

But when at last the time has come
   to put an end to all our pain
You'll come to me, arms open wide
I'll be forever by your side
   And I will live again.

Hilary J Cairns